THE FUNNY SIDE OF
SPORTS

C0-AKC-151

THE FUNNY SIDE OF
SPORTS

Michael J. Pellowski

Illustrated by Sanford Hoffman

Sterling Publishing Co., Inc.
New York

DEDICATION

When the final whistle blows, a true champion's
accomplishments live forever . . .
To Morgan, Matt, Melanie, and Martin with
eternal love

Library of Congress Cataloging-in-Publication Data

Pellowski, Michael.
    The funny side of sports / Michael J. Pellowski ; illustrated by
Sandford Hoffman.
        p.   cm.
    Includes index.
    ISBN 0-8069-3892-7
    1. Sports—Anecdotes.   2. Athletes—Quotations.   3. Sports—Humor.
I. Title.
GV707P446   1996
796'.0207—dc20
                                  95-51511
                                  CIP

1   3   5   7   9   10   8   6   4   2

Published by Sterling Publishing Company, Inc.
387 Park Avenue South, New York, N.Y. 10016
© 1996 by Michael Pellowski
Distributed in Canada by Sterling Publishing
% Canadian Manda Group, One Atlantic Avenue, Suite 105
Toronto, Ontario, Canada M6K 3E7
Distributed in Great Britain and Europe by Cassell PLC
Wellington House, 125 Strand, London WC2R 0BB, England
Distributed in Australia by Capricorn Link (Australia) Pty Ltd.
P.O. Box 6651, Baulkham Hills, Business Centre, NSW 2153, Australia
Manufactured in the United States of America
All rights reserved

Sterling ISBN 0-8069-3892-7

CONTENTS

CRAZY SPORTS QUOTES, COMMENTS, AND CHATTER

JOB JOKE

M. K. Turk, the basketball coach at Southern Mississippi, was talking to Steve Hatchell, the executive director of football's Orange Bowl, in 1990. "Let me see," said Turk, "your job is to pick one team for one day to play in one game and you spend 365 days doing it. Do you have another job like that?"

FINE LINE

Sportscaster Lesley Visser graded Washington Redskins General Manager Charley Casserly's wheeling and dealing on player personnel in 1992 by saying, "Casserly deserves an A for his Plan B acquisitions."

RADIO DIZ JOCKEY

Former president Gerald Ford is an ex-jock who played college football at the University of Michigan in his younger days. However, the ex-president may have made one block too many when he was an offensive center. He once told sports reporters he was an avid baseball fan and then added, "I watch a lot of games on the radio."

DIET CRAZE

Professional golfer Chi Chi Rodriguez once told reporters he eats steak every day. "They say red meat is bad for you, but I never saw a sick-looking tiger," Rodriguez explained.

LIGHT RUNNING

In 1989 junior-lightweight boxer John-John Molina went for a short training run and ended up ten miles from the hotel where his manager, Lou Duva, was waiting. Molina called Duva from a pay phone and complained, "You said run to the red light. All the lights we saw were green."

HOMER

New York Mets baseball broadcaster Ralph Kiner made this crazy comment during a home game at Shea Stadium. "The reason the Mets have played so well at Shea Stadium this season," announced Kiner, "is that they have the best home record in baseball."

TEST CASE

Tom McElroy, a senior associate commissioner of the powerful Big East College Basketball League, had this to say about team schedules in 1995. "You don't schedule a school like Georgetown after exams. You schedule Little Sisters of the Poor."

STRIKE TREE!

Bowler Don Carter was asked his opinion of golf. "One of the advantages of bowling over golf," said Carter, "is that you seldom lose a bowling ball."

COOL RECEPTION

Jack Kent Cooke was the owner of the National Hockey League's Los Angeles Kings team in 1972. That year the Kings had dismal attendance figures. When questioned about the team's drawing power with the fans, Cooke answered, "There are 800,000 Canadians living in the Los Angeles area and I've just learned why they left Canada. They hate hockey!"

NOVEL ANSWER

A critic charged that author James Michener had no sense of tragedy. In reply, Michener fired back, "Anyone who is a lifetime Philadelphia Phillies fan acquires a sense of tragedy."

CLOUD COVER

Pittsburgh Steelers running back Rocky Bleier often talked about how confident his NFL coach, Chuck Noll, was. "He's the only person I know," Bleier said, "who bought an airplane before he learned to fly."

AIRHEADS?

Paul Petzoldt won fame as a mountain climber. Paul's sister was asked why it is that people like to climb mountains. Ms. Petzoldt replied, "They want to get to the top and let the air rush through the holes in their heads!"

MUSIC MAN

Oakland Raiders quarterback Ken Stabler enjoyed going out on the town during his playing days. Asked about his fun-loving lifestyle years ago when he joined the Houston Oilers, Stabler said, "There's nothing wrong with reading the game plan by the light of a jukebox."

HEAD INJURY

Former president Lyndon Johnson made this comment about Congressman Gerald Ford years before Ford became president. Referring to Ford's days as a college football player Johnson cracked, "He played too many times without his helmet."

MEAL SQUEAL

National Football League (NFL) placekicker Jim Bakken made this comment about Bob Young, a 280-pound guard. "For his salad," said Bakken, "you just pour vinegar and oil on your lawn and let him graze."

CHILLING FACT

Comedian Rodney Dangerfield once quipped, "I went to a fight the other night and a hockey game broke out."

WHAT?

NHL goaltender Glenn Resch loved to express himself in words, but wasn't always easy to understand. Once while commenting about himself to reporters Resch said, "If I wasn't talking, I wouldn't know what to say."

KICK THAT COMMENT

Ron Newman was the coach of the North American Soccer League's San Diego Sockers in 1981. On that team were 14 players of foreign birth, many of whom could not speak or understand English. When reporters asked Newman about that fact, Newman replied, "A one-legged Chinaman could play for me if he could put the ball in the back of the net."

BASKET CASE

Basketball Hall of Famer Wilt Chamberlain was a super scorer, but a terrible foul shooter. Wilt said this about his confidence problem at the free throw line. "Once I went to a psychiatrist," explained Chamberlain. "After six months the psychiatrist could shoot 10 for 10, but I was still screwed up."

SHOCKING TRUTH

The Southwest Conference decided to use lie detector tests during investigations of recruiting violations in 1975. When he heard about the tests, basketball coach Eddie Sutton of Arkansas said, "If you strapped a couple of coaches I know into a polygraph chair, they'd be electrocuted!"

TIME WILL TELL

Jim Dickey was asked about future prospects for his basketball team when he was hired to coach the Kansas State Wildcats in 1978. "Kansas State hasn't won a Big Eight Conference in 40 years," Dickey said. "If I don't win a championship in that length of time, I'll resign."

DOLLARS AND SENSE

Someone once asked southpaw tennis star Martina Navratilova why she never insured her left arm with Lloyds of London. Referring to the cost of such an insurance policy, Martina said, "They wanted an arm and a leg!"

LABOR ISSUE

College basketball coach George Raveling was asked just how tall his tallest player was. Answered Raveling, "He was born June 6, 7 and 8."

BORING!

Baseball broadcaster Tom Paciorek was asked for his definition of boredom. "It's having to listen to someone talk about himself," Paciorek answered, "when I want to talk about me."

WORN-OUT WORDS

Years ago when shortstop Johnny Logan of the Milwaukee Braves was asked about his team's rebuilding program and its lack of quick success, he stated, "Rome wasn't born in a day."

CHEAP TALK

Famous Chicago Cubs sportscaster Harry Caray was asked what he thought about Richie Allen, a talented ballplayer who had a knack for getting into trouble. Caray replied, "He's a million-dollar talent with a ten-cent brain."

WET WORDS

Bill DeWitt, the general manager of baseball's Cincinnati Reds, was asked how he felt about making the spitball a legal pitch again. After a moment's thought, DeWitt chuckled and answered, "I told Fred Hutchinson (the Reds' manager at the time) that if he thought our pitchers could learn to throw it, we were for it. If not, we're against it."

EARN YOUR KEEP

When reporters asked the immortal Babe Ruth how he felt about the fact that he as a baseball player made more money than Herbert Hoover, the president of the United States, Ruth had a quick response. "Well, I had a better year than he did," Babe quipped.

WEATHER WISE GUY

Equipment manager Shorty Young of the old Milwaukee Braves once looked outside at some ominous clouds and said, "It looks like a Toronto." What he meant, of course, was a tornado!

CATCH PHRASE

Baseball announcer and funny man Bob Uecker is a famous major-league catcher who doesn't do much bragging about his playing days. "I remember my frustrating days as a catcher in Philadelphia," Uecker said. "The general manager told me they had a very young pitching staff and asked me to help the best way I could. He asked me to quit!"

NEW MATH

Disgruntled Dallas Cowboys running back Duane Thomas once said that Cowboys president Tex Schramm was "a liar, a thief and a crook." When Schramm heard about it, he commented, "Two out of three ain't bad."

HOG WILD

Notre Dame coach Lou Holtz was the head football coach at the University of Arkansas in 1978. Holtz once told sports reporters about faithful Arkansas fans. "When we're playing well the fans shout, 'Woo pig, sooey, sooey,'" Lou said, "but when we're playing poorly the fans yell 'Woo pig, phooey, phooey'!"

SCHOOL'S OUT

In 1989 pitcher Mark Guthrie, of the Minnesota Twins, was asked why he enjoyed beating the Toronto Blue Jays more than the Seattle Mariners. At the time Toronto was leading the American League's East Division, while Seattle was stuck near the bottom of the standings in the West Division. "It's like getting an A in calculus," said Guthrie, "instead of P.E."

FANNED

Football coach Dennis Erickson was once asked to give his definition of a fan. Erickson said, "It's a guy who sits on the forty, criticizes the coaches and players, and has all the answers. Then he leaves the stadium and can't find his car."

HOLD IT!

In 1971 John Brodie was one of the top-paid players in the NFL. In addition to calling signals for his team, John also held the football for P.A.T.s (Point After Attempts). When someone asked Brodie why a million-dollar quarterback had to hold the ball for extra points, he replied, "Well, if I didn't, it would fall over."

BIG SPENDER

Philadelphia Phillies pitcher Tug McGraw was asked how he intended to use his $75,000 salary in 1975. Said Tug wisely, "Ninety percent I'll spend on good times, women, and Irish whiskey. The other ten percent I'll probably waste."

CATCH THAT?

Catcher Tom McCarver, of the Philadelphia Phillies, caught all of pitcher Steve Carlton's games in 1977, which prompted McCarver to say, "When Steve and I die, we're going to be buried in the same cemetery sixty feet, six inches apart." (This is the distance between the pitcher and catcher in baseball.)

HEARING PROBLEM

Major league baseball commissioner Albert "Happy" Chandler told everyone that the only person who could out-talk him was his wife, Mildred. "Once I told a friend I hadn't spoken to my wife in two weeks," Chandler said. "When the friend replied he was shocked to hear that anyone could be so mean, I explained that since I'm a gentleman, I didn't want to interrupt her."

CHILDHOOD DREAM

Steve Owen, a coach for the NFL football Giants, said, "The older we get, the faster we ran as a boy."

WEIGHT UNTIL THE SUN SHINES

Art Donovan, a 300-pound-plus NFL lineman, once described himself as a light eater. "As soon as it's light, I start to eat," said Donovan.

CHEER FEAR

Running back Franco Harris had a super Super Bowl in 1975. Harris, of the Pittsburgh Steelers, broke the single-game rushing record set by Miami Dolphins back Larry Csonka the year before. After the game, reporters asked Csonka about Harris's feat, which Larry saw on television. "I was sitting there rooting for Franco Harris to break the record because he's such a heckuva guy," said Larry. "And all of a sudden, I thought, 'Hey, no, you don't! That's my record you're breaking!' "

FOOD FOR THOUGHT

Nate Newton, a 320-pound-plus tackle in the NFL, once said this about his endless quest to lose weight: "Every night I tell myself I'm going to dream about my girl, I'm going to dream about my girl. But it's always the same dream—ham hocks!"

GAME CLAIM

Many NFL historians believe that the 1958 NFL championship game between the Baltimore Colts and the New York Giants which was won by the Colts in sudden-death overtime was the greatest pro football game ever played. Years later when Jim Lee Howell, who had coached the Giants that year, was asked about that game, he had this to say: "Hell, I never thought it was a great game. We lost, didn't we?"

PLATE FATE

In 1964, a policeman stopped the car of American League baseball player Dick Stuart and asked him why his car still had 1963 license plates. The Boston Red Sox player replied, "I had such a good year I didn't want to forget it."

TO THE POINT

French fencer Eric Srecki won a gold medal in the épée event at the 1992 Olympic Games in Barcelona, Spain. He also won a gold medal at the Olympic Games in Seoul, South Korea, years earlier. Both times, there were few spectators on hand to witness his triumphs. When asked about the lack of fan support for the sport of fencing, Srecki had these amusing comments:

"I understand the problem," he said. "Our sport is just too quick. Most people don't understand it, and before they can ask what happened, the match is over. Maybe if we dueled to the death, more fans would watch. But then there would be fewer people going for the gold, and think how lonely the victory stand would be with just one person on it."

STOP IT

NHL goalie Don Beaupre stood five feet, eight inches tall and weighed 155 pounds. A reporter asked him how a man of his small size could play in the National Hockey League.

"I just have to stop the puck," replied Beaupre, "not beat it up!"

THINK STINK

Norm Van Brocklin, the famous NFL quarterback and coach, wasn't very fond of sports reporters who bombarded him with pesky questions. In 1979 Norm underwent brain surgery. When reporters asked him about the operation, Van Brocklin answered, "It was a brain transplant. I got a sportswriter's brain so I could be sure that I got one that hadn't been used."

SICK COMMENT

NFL coach Jerry Glanville had a bout with pneumonia in 1990. Talking about the symptoms, Coach Glanville joked, "I thought maybe I was going to become a general manager because I kept wanting to take a nap."

BE SEATED

New York Giants football coach Allie Sherman said this about the learning process: "The mind can absorb only what the seat can endure."

CASEY AT BANTER

Casey Stengel was a major league baseball player and manager for many years. He is fondly remembered as baseball's wacky wizard of words.

Sensible Pick

When Casey was the manager of the New York Mets in 1961, he helped select catcher Hobie Landrith in the expansion draft. Asked why he picked Landrith, Stengel replied, "If you don't have a catcher, you have a lot of passed balls."

Retirement Plan

When asked about possible plans for retirement, Casey Stengel replied, "Most people my age are dead!"

Close Shave

After a team managed by Casey lost a doubleheader to a weak opponent, Stengel went into a barber shop.

"Give me a shave," he told the barber.

"Anything else?" asked the barber.

"Yes," said Casey. "Don't cut my throat. I may want to do that later myself."

Catch Phrase

Casey had this to say about catcher Chris Canizzaro: "He's the only defensive catcher in baseball who can't catch!"

THE BUTT OF JOKES

In 1990, Tony Campbell, a guard for the NBA Minnesota Timberwolves, fell on his hip during a game against the Washington Bullets and suffered a painful injury. After the game Campbell said, "My gluteus maximus is hurteus enormous."

GIANT KILLER

Television sportscaster Dick Schaap once said, "For the New York Giants, the worst time of the year is the football season."

RETIRE QUICK

Abe Lemons was 67 years old when he decided to retire as the head basketball coach at Oklahoma City University at the end of the 1989–90 season. When a reporter asked Abe just when he finally decided to retire, Lemons cracked, "When I saw my team play."

CASH COURSE

David Stern, NBA commissioner, signed a five year contract worth $27.5 million dollars in 1990. When Pat Williams, the general manager of the Orlando Magic, heard about Stern's deal, he quipped, "All I know is that on airplane trips, David's wallet will be considered carry-on baggage."

HELP WANTED

University of Georgia basketball center Arlando Bennett broke his arm in 1989 and had to wear a cast. At the team's training table Bennett asked a teammate to help him cut up his meat. "When you're a low-post player," Arlando said, "you always need someone to feed you."

HEAVY THINKER

Rotund comedian Jackie Leonard once said to slim jockey Willie Shoemaker, "I lost more pounds than you are."

CHILL OUT!

When Rod Gilbert was a star player in the NHL, he was asked if hockey fights were faked. "If they were faked," answered Gilbert, "you'd see me in more of them."

SIT-DOWN STRIKE

Heavyweight Ken Norton knocked out opposing fighter Duane Bobick in the first round of their 1977 prizefight. When questioned about the contest, former welterweight champ Curtis Cokes said, "It's a shame for a man to train six weeks and not even get to use his stool."

YIPES

NBA basketball star Jayson Williams had this to say about himself in 1994: "Heaven don't want me and hell's scared I'm going to take over."

CRUDDY BUDDY

Baseball stars Graig Nettles and Reggie Jackson both played for the New York Yankees in 1978. When asked about being teammates with Jackson, Nettles replied, "The advantage is in getting to watch Reggie Jackson play every day. The disadvantage is getting to watch Reggie Jackson play every day."

CHEERS

When former major league baseball pitcher Bob Lemon was asked about his playing days, he joking replied, "I had my bad days on the field, but I didn't take them home with me. I left them in a bar along the way."

DIGGER THIS

When sportscaster Digger Phelps was a college basketball coach, he made the following comment: "I would like to deny the statement that I think basketball is a matter of life and death," said Phelps. "It's more important than that."

LIGHTS OUT

"Why don't you enforce a curfew for your team?" someone asked college basketball coach Abe Lemons. "The reason I don't have a curfew," replied Lemons, "is that it's always your star who gets caught."

SWINGER

Utility player Woodie Held, who played baseball in the major leagues from 1954 to 1969, once gave this batting tip to a young slugger. "Don't forget to swing hard," advised Held, "in case you hit the ball."

IF THE GLOVE FITS

Baseball slugger Floyd "Babe" Herman was a terrific hitter but a lousy fielder. Teammate Fresco Thompson had this to say about Babe's defensive ability: "Babe wore a glove for only one reason. It was a league custom. A glove would last him a minimum of six years because it rarely made contact with the ball."

DOCTOR UP THE FIELD

After infielder Bobby Brown left major league baseball to become a doctor, his old teammate Gene Woodling said this about Brown's fielding: "He had such lousy hands when he played third, I wouldn't want him to operate on me!"

INFIELDER CHATTER

Shortstop Johnny Logan, of the Milwaukee Braves, had a wacky way with words. When Logan was advised that an item about him in a newspaper was a typographical error, he yelled, "The hell it was. It was a clean base hit!"

BRIGHT SPOT—NOT!

How bad a fielder was Los Angeles Dodgers hurler Billy Loes? According to sportscaster Joe Garagiola, "Billy Loes was the only player in the majors who could lose a ground ball in the sun."

PIE-FACED

Johnny Logan was in a Milwaukee restaurant one evening and wanted dessert. "I'll have pie à la mode with ice cream," ordered Johnny.

TICKED OFF

Sportswriter Melvin Durslag had this to say about Los Angeles Dodgers shortstop Bill Russell's ability to make fielding plays: "I've seen better hands on a clock!"

CHANGE

Sports commentator Howard Cosell said this about former Dodgers owner Walter O'Malley, referring to O'Malley's handling of his team: "The man has a cash register where his heart should be."

DUCK, GRANNY!

Pitcher Johnny Allen, who spent many years in major league baseball with various teams, wasn't afraid to knock down a batter with a pitch in certain key situations. When someone asked Allen if he'd knock down his grandmother in the clutch, Johnny gave an honest reply: "I don't guess I'd go that far, but I sure wouldn't give her a good ball to hit!"

TALL TALE

Immortal baseball manager Miller Huggins was asked what a hitter in a slump needs most. Cracked Huggins with a smile, "A string of good alibis."

TUNNEL VISION

Notre Dame football coach Lou Holtz once made this comment about progress: "Sometimes the light at the end of a tunnel is an oncoming train."

WHO'S THE BOSS?

A sports reporter once said, "Only in pro sports do we keep the temperamental employee and fire the boss."

FAST TALK

A young track sprinter asked famous track coach Dink Templeton how he could improve his time in the 100-yard dash. "Just run faster," grunted Templeton.

STOMACH TROUBLE

A reporter asked immortal NBA coach Red Auerbach if he ever got ulcers when he coached in the league. "I didn't get ulcers," replied Auerbach. "I gave them!"

FOOTBALL FOLLIES

SOFT SOAP

"The coach just handed me a bar of soap," a rookie quarterback said to a veteran center. "What does it mean?"

"Sonny," said the veteran, "it means you've been demoted to the scrub team."

MEAL DEAL

Defensive tackle Roosevelt Grier, of the New York Giants, often had trouble keeping his weight down to where his head coach, Allie Sherman, wanted it. "Rosie," as he was called, usually tipped the scales at 330 pounds and Allie wanted him to weigh in at around 285 pounds. To help Grier with his dieting, Allie Sherman told him to use a food-replacement diet drink to curb his appetite during the off-season. Rosie was supposed to drink it instead of eating.

When it was time for the football season to begin, Rosie showed up at the Giants' training camp more overweight than ever. Coach Allie Sherman was flabbergasted. "What happened to the diet?" he yelled. "Didn't you try to lose weight? What about the diet drink?"

Rosie Grier sighed and looked his coach right in the eye. "Coach, I did try!" he insisted. "I did drink that replacement drink you gave me. In fact," he added, "I got to liking it a lot. I liked it so much that I drank three or four cans of it with every meal."

CASH COURSE

Running back Preston Pearson was a member of the Dallas Cowboys football team that lost 35-31 to the Pittsburgh Steelers in Super Bowl XIII. Pearson, who once played for the Steelers, continued to live in Pittsburgh with his wife during the off-season. After the Cowboys' loss, Mrs. Pearson went to her local bank in Pittsburgh to deposit her husband's Super Bowl check and was told by a teller that for a deposit of that size she was entitled to a free gift the bank was offering. The gift was a record album which featured a review of the Steelers' championship season and a recording of their fight song. As you might expect, she refused to accept it.

OH, BROTHER!

The 1982 Super Bowl produced an interesting moment in NFL history. When San Francisco 49ers kicker Ray Wersching booted a squib kick, Cincinnati Bengals running back Archie Griffin attempted to catch it. Archie bobbled the ball, fumbling it back to his brother and fellow running back, Ray Griffin. Ray also bobbled the ball, fumbling it to Milt McColl of the 49ers, who recovered it. The incident was the NFL's first case of brotherly butterfingers.

TOUGH TALK

An offensive lineman on the Cleveland Browns squad in 1991 didn't have much respect for his teammates who played in the defensive secondary. When asked to describe the Browns defensive backs, he said, "Our defensive backs are like a river. There's more activity at the mouth than at the source."

THAT PLAY STINKS

Years ago, pro football official Harry Robb angered the Pittsburgh Steelers squad by calling penalty after penalty against them. After yet another offside call went against the Steelers, Pittsburgh center Chuck Cherundolo lost his temper. "Hey, Robb! You stink, pal," he shouted.

Harry Robb said nothing, picked up the football, and marched off an additional 15-yard penalty. When he had reached the appropriate distance, he put the ball down and looked back at Chuck. "Hey, Cherundolo," he shouted at the irate center. "How do I smell from here?"

HARD-HEADED

Football Hall of Fame running back Bronko Nagurski was one of the toughest men to ever play the game. One afternoon while playing for the Chicago Bears, he was handed the ball and promptly headed towards the sidelines. Putting his head down and running full-speed without watching where he was going, he crashed head-first into a steel-and-concrete dugout. He fell to the ground stunned and dazed. The first thing he said when he came to minutes later was, "Boy, that last guy sure hit me hard!"

RHYME TIME

A would-be football poet once wrote, "To go unbeaten and gain lasting fame, better not schedule Notre Dame."

TAKE IT SITTING DOWN

Renowned football coach Knute Rockne liked to quiz his players about team strategy. One day he had his players huddle around him and he singled out a rookie quarterback for interrogation.

"It's the third quarter," Rockne roared. "We have the ball. It's second down with two yards to go at our own 20 yard line. What do you do?"

"Me?" gasped the surprised rookie.

"Yes, you!" barked Rockne.

"Well," muttered the young quarterback. "I'd just slide down the bench to get a better look at the next play."

SNOOZE ALARM

After his team chalked up a 70-30 win, football coach Hugh Campbell of Whitworth College in Spokane, Washington, was questioned about the victory.

"It wasn't as easy as you think," Hugh said. "It's hard to stay awake that long."

GUIDANCE

When John McKay was coach of the NFL Tampa Bay Buccaneers, someone asked him if his teams pray for victory. Said McKay, "God's busy. They have to make do with me."

ROUGH SPORT

Tempers sometimes flare during a football game and fights result. However, tempers really got out of hand at the 1978 meeting between Colorado State and Wyoming on the gridiron. The two football teams got into a brawl during the opening coin toss!

FIGHT NICE

After the New York Jets and the New England Patriots got into a huge brawl during their NFL meeting in 1980, Patriots coach Ron Erhardt was asked about the fines levied by the league on all individuals involved in the altercation. "The money goes to a good cause," Ron explained. "It goes to the retirement fund of the coaches in the league." Erhardt then smiled and added, "That's why when the fight broke out I waved the whole squad onto the field."

KILLER STATEMENT

"Coach, what do you think of your team's execution?" a reporter asked Tampa Bay coach John McKay after a Buccaneer loss to the Cleveland Browns. "I think it's a good idea," the coach fired back.

UNBALANCED ATTACK

When Ron Enright was coach of the South Carolina football team, his squad faced a Clemson team that had some huge players. When reporters asked Enright about the size of the Clemson squad, Ron said, "Those boys are so big that every time they run out on the field they tip it to one side."

GULP!

When coach Sam Rutigliano's Cleveland Browns received a lot of publicity for making the playoffs in 1980, he was asked if all the notoriety worried him. "No," said Sam. "Publicity is just like poison. It's okay as long as you don't swallow it."

FIZZ!

A banner strung up at Super Bowl XVI read, "We're here just for the beer!"

I SWEAR

Long ago, Frank Szymanski, a center for the Notre Dame basketball team, appeared in court as a witness. Szymanski swore to tell the truth, the whole truth, and nothing but the truth.

"What position do you play at Notre Dame?" the judge asked.

"Center, your honor."

"How good a center are you?"

"Judge," Frank answered, "I'm the best center Notre Dame ever had."

Sitting in the audience was Szymanski's coach at Notre Dame, Frank Leahy. Leahy was surprised by Szymanski's comment because the young center was known to be very modest. After court ended Leahy asked him about his boast. "How could you make a statement about yourself in public like that?" Frank Szymanski just shrugged. "I had to, Coach. I was under oath," he explained.

FAST GETAWAY

A reporter once asked LaVell Edwards, the football coach at Brigham Young University, if he preferred speed or quickness in his wide receivers. LaVell thought for a minute and then said, "I'd like them to have both, but if they had both they'd be at the University of Southern California."

CATCH PHRASE

During the 1946 Army-Notre Dame football game, safety Arnold Tucker of Army intercepted three passes thrown by Notre Dame quarterback Johnny Lujack. Since Lujack was famous for his passing accuracy, Notre Dame coach Frank Leahy was puzzled.

"Tell me, John," Leahy said. "Why did you throw so many passes to Tucker?"

Johnny Lujack grinned and shrugged his shoulders. "He was the only man open, coach," replied Lujack.

HAIR TODAY, GONE TOMORROW

Placekicker Pat Leahy, of the New York Jets, was having a conversation with a sportswriter who thought he knew all about football. "The legs are the first thing to go on an old athlete," said the sportswriter.

Pat Leahy disagreed. "The legs aren't the first thing to go on an athlete," he said. "It's the hair."

PRAY FOR VICTORY

A football game between Notre Dame, a Catholic college, and Southern Methodist, a Protestant university, was about to begin. A football fan arrived late and took his seat in the stands between a priest who'd graduated from Notre Dame and a minister who'd graduated from Southern Methodist. "Who are you rooting for?" the priest asked the fan. The man looked at the priest and then glanced at the minister.

"I don't care who wins," he admitted. "I just came to enjoy the game."

"Oh," grunted the minister to the priest as he pointed at the man. "He's an atheist!"

GUN SHY

Running back Barry Sanders, of the Detroit Lions, has been almost unstoppable during his NFL career and opposing coaches know it. When linebacker coach Dave McGinnis, of the Chicago Bears, was asked how he would halt the Lions' potent offensive attack, he came up with an interesting plan. "The key to Detroit's run and shoot offense is Barry Sanders," said McGinnis. He then added with a smile, "When Barry runs, you shoot him!"

HOOP SCOOPS

PRIZE PUPIL

One of the door prizes at the 1966 NBA All-Star luncheon was a copy of a book entitled *Play Better Basketball,* written by great NBA guard Oscar Robertson. The winner of the prize was a pretty good player, too. It was great NBA center Wilt Chamberlain!

LOW GRADE

A basketball player on the 1965 Texas A & M squad took his grade printout to Coach Shelby Metcalf for examination. To his dismay, Coach Metcalf looked at the printout and saw that the player had four F's and one D.

"Son," he said, "it looks to me like you're spending too much time on one subject."

GOING COURTING

When Frank Layden was coach of the Utah Jazz, someone asked him how tough his old high school team in Brooklyn was. Frank grinned and said, "We had nicknames like Scarface and Toothless—and those were just the cheerleaders."

DON'T LISTEN

Louie Carnesecca, who coached both in college and the pros, was one of basketball's most colorful and energetic personalities. Louie had a habit of getting very emotional during court contests. He would yell, scream, and holler at his players as they raced up and down. Finally, one day after a very close game that luckily resulted in a win for Louie's St. John's University Redmen, a reporter asked him about his ranting and raving on the sidelines. "Why waste all that energy?" the reporter asked. "The players on the court can't hear what you're yelling at them anyway."

Louie calmly looked at the reporter and replied, "Thank God."

SMART GUYS

An inquisitive gentleman once asked Harvard basketball coach Peter Roby about his recruiting procedure. "If I ask a kid how he did on the boards," replied Roby, "and he says, 'Twelve a game,' I know he's *not* coming to Harvard."

SHOT DOWN

NBA star Pete Maravich was one of basketball's greatest scoring machines. Pete had such a great shot that he was nicknamed "Pistol Pete." However, even a pistol can fire blanks once in a while, and that's just what happened to Maravich one rare evening. He fired and missed and fired and missed until his coach finally yanked him out of the game. "Don't take me out," Pete said. "We're losing. We need shooters out there."

The coach took a long look at Pistol Pete. "Not shooters," he corrected. "Scorers!"

YOU WHO?

Al Menendez was the New Jersey Nets' color man for the Nets' radio broadcasts in 1981. At the time, he lived with his mother. When the Nets played the New York Knicks for the first time that season, she stayed home to listen to her son do the game on the radio. After the game, Al went home and asked her, "How did I do?"

"It was good, but it didn't sound like you," his mom answered. When Al checked the setting on her radio dial, he found that she had listened to the game broadcast by the New York Knick commentators on a rival radio station!

WELCOME, STRANGERS

For the longest time, tiny Franconia College in New Hampshire did not have a home court for its basketball team to play on. The team had to play all of its hoop contests on the road. To make the players feel more at home wherever they played, masterminds at Franconia came up with a great idea. The college adopted the nickname "Visitors" for its basketball team. From then on, wherever the Visitors played, they saw their name on the opposing team's scoreboard.

TRAVELLING MUSIC

Basketball superstar Michael Jordan, of the Chicago Bulls, was asked why he chose geography as his college major while at the University of North Carolina. Answered Michael, "I knew that I would be going places someday and I just wanted to know where I was when I got there."

TOAST

Theresa Grentz is acknowledged to be one of the best college coaches of women's basketball in the United States. She has been an Olympic coach and guided the Lady Scarlet Knights of Rutgers University to a national title. Way back in 1974, Grentz was starting out as the coach of little St. Joseph's University in Pennsylvania. One night back then, she heard a knock at her office door. When she opened it she saw an elderly priest. He wanted to make her a gift of a bottle of Scotch whiskey as a welcoming present. "Thank you,' said Theresa, "but I don't drink."

"Honey," said the priest with a twinkle in his eye. "If you stay in the profession, you might."

CLASS PASS

During the 1978 basketball season, Andy Furman, the sports information director at Oral Roberts University, wanted to make sure his hoop team always played before a sizeable home crowd, so he cooked up interesting ways to pack the stands. When ORU played the Bulgarian national team, Furman gave free passes to anyone of Bulgarian ancestry living around Tulsa, Oklahoma. Later in the season, when Oral Roberts played Hardin-Simmons University, he gave free passes to individuals with the last names of Hardin or Simmons.

WHAT DO YOU KNOW?

Noted sports attorney Bob Woolf was college basketball superstar Larry Bird's agent when the Boston Celtics made Bird their number-one draft pick. Negotiations between Woolf and the Celtics' management did not go smoothly and Bird remained unsigned much too long as far as the Boston fans were concerned. During the time when negotiations seemed at a dead end, Bob Woolf was driving through Worcester, Massachusetts, when he took a wrong turn and got lost. He stopped his car at a red light and called out to the driver of the auto next to him. "Hey, fella," said Woolf, "how do I get to Boston?"

The driver of the other car looked at Bob and recognized him. "Hey! You're Bob Woolf, right?" Woolf nodded. "When's Larry Bird going to sign with the Celtics?" the man asked impatiently.

Woolf shrugged his shoulders. "I don't know," he answered honestly, as the light changed from red to green.

"Well, then I don't know how to get to Boston," the driver of the other car yelled as he pulled away.

SMALL TALK

George Mikan was the first big man to truly dominate the game of basketball in both college and the NBA. At 6 feet 9 inches tall, Big George didn't have many equals on the court during the 1940's and 1950's. However, he did hear some big talk from others during his playing days. One of his favorite zingers came from referee Sid Borgia during the 1954 NBA All-Star Game at New York's Madison Square Garden. George was playing for the West All-Stars. His team was down by two points when he was fouled at the end of the game with no time remaining on the clock. He needed to make both foul shots to keep his team alive. Sid Borgia, who only stood as high as Mikan's waist, handed him the ball and said, "Okay, Big George, you're always telling me I choke under pressure. Now I'm going to stand here and watch you choke." George smiled and calmly sank the two shots that tied the contest and sent the game into overtime. However, Sid did have the last smirk. The East All-Stars ended up winning the game in overtime.

GETTING TECHNICAL

When college referee Bob Hammel officiated at a game between the University of Nebraska and the University of Oklahoma, Coach John MacLeod of Oklahoma complained about the job Hammel was doing.

"I can't call a technical foul on something I didn't see," Hammel said to MacLeod after a supposed infraction.

"Why not?" asked MacLeod. "You've been calling them that way all night."

STRAIGHT TALK

Bob Harding was a top sportswriter for a New Jersey newspaper for a quarter of a century. He was a well-respected and widely read reporter during the 1960's and 1970's, covering professional basketball for his paper in the days when television interviews with pro athletes were few and far between. Of course people who read Bob's column had no idea that he stuttered.

At the same time, an NBA superstar named Bob Love was making headlines as a member of the Chicago Bulls. Because television interviews were scarce, no one realized Bob Love also stuttered.

When the Chicago Bulls played in New York, Bob Harding arranged to have an interview with Bob Love. When the men met face to face and sat down to do the interview, trouble started. Bob Harding stuttered as he asked Bob Love the first question. Instantly, Love got angry because he thought Harding was ridiculing him. Angrily, he stuttered his response. It was then Harding's turn to get angry. He thought Bob Love was thoughtlessly making fun of *him*. After a few more questions and responses, both men were on the verge of losing their temper. They stood up and started shouting at each other. It was then that a New York Knicks publicity man named Frankie Blauschild, who was on hand for the interview, let the cat out of the bag. "Hey, cool it, you guys," he yelled. "You both have the same speech problem." Bob Harding and Bob Love exchanged glances and then broke into laughter.

SILLY SUPERSTITIONS AND JERKY JINXES

LEFT OUT

Hockey players Robert Picard and Guy Charron were superstitious about how they prepared to play a NHL game: Both men always put on their left pieces of equipment first. NHL player Ryan Walter wasn't quite as superstitious as Picard and Charron: He believed he'd have good luck as long as he put on his left skate before his right one.

NUMBER, PLEASE

Soccer superstar Pelé, from Brazil, believed the number ten was his lucky number. He always wore that number as a player and stayed in hotel rooms and had automobile license plates that used combinations of it (such as 1010).

SOCK IT TO ME

Olympic athlete Bruce Jenner wore a pair of old white socks that had a black stripe at the top in every competition he was in over a five-year span because he thought the socks were good luck. Maybe Jenner's superstition wasn't so silly, because he won a gold medal in the decathlon at the 1976 Olympics while wearing his much darned lucky socks.

MONEY MAN

Pro golfer Tom Weiskopf believes he will have good luck on the links if he carries three coins in his pocket.

SHOT CLOCKED

NBA superstar Nate "Tiny" Archibald would never leave the court before a game until after he made his final warmup shot. A missed shot meant bad luck.

YUK!

During a successful hitting streak, major league catcher Al Lopez ate kippered herring and eggs for breakfast 17 days in a row because he thought changing his morning routine might jinx him.

BATTY BOY

Major leaguer Joe Gordon would change bats every time he'd go to the plate to hit—just for luck.

GET YOUR GOAT

In 1945, William Sianis put a hex on the Chicago Cubs baseball team because the club wouldn't let Sianis bring his pet goat into Wrigley Field for a World Series game. The hex was supposed to keep the Cubs from ever winning a pennant. In 1981, William Sianis's son Sam finally lifted the hex. Why? The Cubs invited Sam to attend a game at Wrigley Field along with a goat named Billy, who was the mascot of the popular Chicago tavern owned by the Sianis family. It was all part of a clever publicity stunt.

NO THROW

Major league third baseman Joe Dugan believed it was bad luck for him to throw a baseball to a pitcher standing on the mound. Dugan would only throw the ball to a pitcher for a putout. On all other occasions, Dugan would carry the ball from third to the mound and hand it to the pitcher.

SCREWY CHEWY

Past baseball star Eddie Collins thought it lucky to stick a wad of well-chewed gum on the button of his baseball cap when he went to the plate to hit. (In those days, players did not wear helmets.) If Collins got two strikes, he thought it even luckier to remove the gum from his cap, pop it into his mouth, and chew it.

SWING THING

Former Dodgers All-Star first baseman Steve Garvey had a superstition about batting. He always took the same number of practice swings before a pitch.

CLOAK, NO JOKE!

Heavyweight champ Muhammad Ali always wore a "lucky" robe for his important fights. The robe was a present to him from rock immortal Elvis Presley.

TOWELS, PLEASE!

When basketball sportscaster Tom Young was a college coach he never directed his team without having a towel clenched in his hands. Former NBA star Bill Bradley, who later became a U.S. senator, insisted a towel be only put on his right shoulder during time-outs, when he was a New York Knick player.

SHOWER POWER!

Pro baseball player Minnie Minoso, of the Chicago White Sox, blamed his batting slump during a double-header on "evil spirits" in his uniform. To get rid of the bad spirits, Minoso took a shower while wearing his uniform and washed away the evil. In the next game, Minoso got three hits—two of them home runs!

POCKET PROBLEM

Hurler Dizzy Trout absolutely refused to pitch in a major league game unless a red bandanna was tucked in his hip pocket.

THUMB LUCK

Lots of pro bowlers believe it is good luck to blow into the thumb hole of the ball before rolling it. Now, that's a lot of hot air!

P.U.!

Basketball coach Al McGuire wore the same lucky blue suit so long during a Marquette winning streak in 1977 that the smell of the suit turned up the noses of players sitting next to him on the bench.

BIRD BRAIN

Just for luck, pro tennis player Art Larsen used to talk to an imaginary eagle which he said was perched on his right shoulder during matches. The bird supposedly brought him good luck.

HATS OFF

Football coach Curly Lambeau, of the Green Bay Packers, wore a different hat to every game his team played. He believed that wearing the same hat two games in a row was bad luck.

SHUT UP!

Major league baseball player Chico Salmon was extremely superstitious. He was so afraid of evil spirits that he not only bolted the door to his hotel room every night, but also covered up every opening to the outside and always slept with all the lights on.

IF IT SUITS YOU

During a Brooklyn Dodgers 15-game winning streak in 1954, team manager Leo Durocher wore the same black shoes, grey slacks, blue coat, and knitted blue tie every single day during the streak because he didn't want to "wash away" the good luck.

DOUBLE TROUBLE

NBA star John "Hondo" Havlicek, of the Boston Celtics, never left the floor before a game until he made his *last two* warmup shots.

SHOE THING

Pro boxers Willie Pep and Willie Pastrano shared a superstition. They both believed it was good luck to tie their wedding ring to their shoelaces for a prizefight.

PENNYWISE

Golfer Lee Elder carries a penny given to him by his wife for luck when he first joined the pro tour. He uses the penny to mark his ball on golf courses.

FRIDAY THE 13TH? HA!

Who says Friday the 13th is bad luck? Pro golfer Andy Bean was born on Friday the 13th, as was golfer Tom Watson's daughter Meg.

KISSEY! KISSEY!

Big league slugger Gil Hodges had the sweet habit of always throwing a kiss in the direction of where his wife sat in the stands whenever he hit a home run.

CAT'S OUT OF THE BAG

Heavyweight boxer Ken Norton hated the sight of black cats and considered them extremely unlucky.

SODA SHOCK

NFL offensive lineman George Buehler believed it was good luck to practice blocking a soda machine inside his team's locker room just before game time.

LUCKY BABE

Babe Ruth was super-superstitious. His dressing area was always adorned with wooden horseshoes, miniature totem poles, jade monkeys, and other lucky charms.

ON A BARREL ROLE

A crazy old baseball superstition concerned empty beer barrels. Baseball players of the past believed that seeing a truckload of empty beer barrels going by before a game was good luck and guaranteed a team would get a lot of hits. To take advantage of that silly superstition, manager John McGraw of the New York Giants once secretly hired a man to drive a truck filled with empty beer barrels past his team as the players entered the stadium for a crucial series against the Chicago Cubs. McGraw's trick worked, as the truck rolled past the Giant players before each contest of the four-game series. However, the secret was uncovered after the series' end when the truck driver showed up at the stadium looking to be paid for services rendered.

PHIL THE CHILL

NHL hockey great Phil Esposito was another pro athlete who believed in the value of lucky charms. His locker was always crammed full of Italian charms, religious medals, and a red metal emblem in the shape of a heart sent to him by an Oriental woman.

LUCKY HIT

The old Brooklyn Dodgers were in the middle of a losing streak when Dodger Frenchy Bordagaray threw a ball and accidentally hit Brooklyn manager Casey Stengel on the head during pregame practice. Casey was mad about getting conked, but didn't say much. The Dodgers broke their losing streak by winning that day. After the game, a supersitious Bordagaray went up to Stengel and suggested a way to keep the new lucky streak intact. He proposed that he bean the Dodger manager on the head with a ball every game from then on. Casey wasn't superstitious enough to agree to that.

YOU'RE A WIENER

In 1960, the Pittsburgh Pirates had a little help in winning the National League pennant. That help came in the form of a hex the fans used against opposing teams. The hex was called the Green Wienie and it was cooked up by the Pirates' radio announcer, Bob Prince. Prince painted a ballpark frankfurter green and told fans that pointing a green wienie at opposing players and teams would jinx the opposition and bring the Pirates luck. Soon green wienies were seen everywhere in the stands. Pointing the green wienies apparently worked because—hot dog!—the Pirates did win the pennant and the World Series.

BASEBALL BELLY LAUGHS

One very hot summer afternoon major league umpire Jocko Conlon cautioned pitcher Rip Sewell against wiping perspiration off his forehead with his hand. Conlon believed Sewell was trying to throw a spitball. "Hey, Sewell, what you're doing ain't legal," yelled Umpire Conlon. "What ain't legal," Sewell hollered back, "sweating?"

PAY DAZE

In 1989, Chicago Cubs manager Don Zimmer did a radio commercial for Popeye's Chicken and another one for the Nutri System Diet Plan. When Pittsburgh Pirates manager Jim Leyland heard about the commercials, he smiled and remarked, "Zim gets paid to eat *and* to diet!

GOOD NUDES

After a run of bad luck at the plate, Al Simmons of the old Philadelphia A's took a shower and then absent-mindedly put on his hat—and nothing else. In the next game he got four hits. From then on Simmons practised the good-luck ritual of taking a shower and then putting on a hat while he was naked and dripping wet.

RUN DOWN

The manager of the Texas Rangers went out to the mound to remove his starting pitcher during an American League game in 1979. "But, Skip," protested the pitcher. "I'm not tired."

The manager plucked the ball from the hurler's hand and replied, "No, but the outfielders sure are!"

PITCHER IMPERFECT

Rex Barney was a pitcher for the old Brooklyn Dodgers in the 1940s. How good was Barney? Sportswriter Bob Cooke said it all when he cracked, "Rex Barney would be the league's best pitcher . . . if the plate were high and outside."

ICING ON THE CAKE

Marv Throneberry, the first baseman for the New York Mets in 1962, wasn't known as a great fielder. On Marv's birthday that year teammate Richie Ashburn walked up to Thronberry and shook his hand. "Happy Birthday, Marv," said Ashburn. "We were going to give you a cake, but we thought you'd drop it.

MONEY MATTERS

How much money is there to be made playing major league baseball? The following comment will give you a clue. A pitcher for the Oakland A's once said of his off-season job in a bank. "I don't think I'll continue in banking. There's not enough money in it."

BIG JOKE

Major league umpire Ed Runge was teasing hitter Joe Koppe about his low batting average. "Joe," said Runge, "if someone threw you an elephant you couldn't hit it."

"Ed," Koppe answered, "if someone threw me an elephant you couldn't call it."

TAPS

Brooklyn Dodger Frenchy Bordagaray got on the bad side of his manager, Casey Stengel, one afternoon. Bordagaray was picked off second base even though he'd only taken a short lead. "What happened?" roared Stengel. "How could you get picked off?"

"Gee, I don't know Casey," Frenchy replied. "I was standing near second tapping the base with my foot . . . and I guess they got me between taps."

TIME OUT

New York Mets catcher Mickey Sasser was excused from a game between the Mets and the Montreal Expos to take care of some family business. When the late night game went into extra innings, Sasser ended up returning to the stadium after midnight to see its conclusion. When Mets announcer Ralph Kiner saw Mickey Sasser on the bench, he said, "Sasser arrived tomorrow for today's game."

SHAKE PAL

When rookie pitcher Brian DuBois of the Detroit Tigers saw his manager, Sparky Anderson, come out of the dugout during a game against the Yankees, shout "Time," and walk towards the mound with his right hand extended, DuBois didn't realize that Anderson wanted the ball and was taking him out of the game. Instead of handing Anderson the ball, the confused rookie took the glove off his right hand and proceeded to shake hands with his astonished manager.

RUNNING JOKE

Former major league catcher Joe Garagiola said he once saw a scouting report on himself. It read: "Deceiving runner. He's slower than he looks."

SIGN LANGUAGE

When hurler Vernon "Lefty" Gomez was on the mound for the New York Yankees, he cringed when home-run slugger Jimmy Foxx stepped up to the plate. Catcher Bill Dickey gave Gomez sign after sign which Lefty promptly shook off one after the other. After Gomez refused every pitch in the book, Dickey called time and walked out to the mound. "Just what do you want to throw him?" Bill Dickey asked the pitcher. "To tell you the truth," Lefty replied, "I'd just as soon not throw him anything."

QUICK WIT

"To what do you attribute your great success as a pitcher?" a young sports reporter asked Yankee hurler Lefty Gomez.

"Clean living and a fast outfield," Gomez rapidly replied.

SQUEALER

When New York Yankee scout Al Cuccinello's grandson was five years old, he asked his mother to explain his grandfather's job. "He watches other teams play and then tells the Yankees about it," the boy's mom told him.

"Oh," said the little boy, "you mean Grandpop is a snitcher."

KNUCKLE DOWN

"How do you catch a knuckleball?" a sports reporter asked catcher Bob Uecker one day. Funny guy Uecker replied, "After it stops rolling, I pick it up and throw it back to the pitcher."

FOLLOW THE LEADER

Fiery Frankie Frisch was the player-manager of the St. Louis Cardinals for many years. Frisch liked to give his new players some wise advice during spring training. "Pick out a veteran star on our team and imitate him on the field," Frankie told the newcomers.

After Frisch's pep talk, the team of veterans and rookies went out to practice. Frankie lazily leaned on a bat and watched his squad hustle through various drills. Suddenly he noticed a young rookie named Sam Narron leaning on a bat and doing absolutely nothing. Frisch went wild. "Narron! What are you doing?" he screamed. "How dare you loaf at practice after what I just said? Didn't I tell you to pick out one of our veteran players to imitate on the field?"

Sam Narron looked at his skipper in a confused way. "Yes, sir, and I did," he replied sheepishly. "I picked you to imitate."

BLIND FAITH

Dodger infielder Fresco Thompson was famous for having disputes with umpires. Once a question about a rule came up and Thompson got into his usual argument with the man in blue. "I've got my rule book right here," the ump said to Fresco in an attempt to settle the issue.

"How do you expect me to read that?" the angry Dodger yelled. "If it's your rule book, it must be written in Braille."

WISE CRACK

Detroit Tiger pitcher Paul Foytack was asked if battery mate Red Wilson was a good catcher. "I don't know," replied the Tigers' hurler candidly. "He never caught anything I threw. The batters always got to it first."

SHOE THING

Nippy Jones of the Milwaukee Braves had a reputation for neatness. His uniform was always clean and pressed and his spikes were always shined. In 1957, Nippy's knack for neatness helped the Braves win a World Series game against the Yankees. When Jones came to the plate as a pinch hitter, he claimed that a pitched ball hit him on the foot and he was entitled to first base. Home plate umpire Augie Donatelli didn't believe him, but when Jones asked the umpire to check the ball for a smudge of shoe polish to support his claim, the polish was on the ball. Nippy Jones went to first, the play ignited a Braves' rally, and Milwaukee went on to win the game—which proves that even in baseball neatness sometimes counts.

HIT PARADE

"How do you p　　1 to Ty Cobb?" someone once asked hurler Walter Johnson, one of baseball's greatest pitchers. "I just throw him my best pitch," Johnson replied, "and then I run over and back up third base."

GETTING RATTLED

Dizzy Dean was called out on a close play at first and tried to get into an argument with the umpire. "I was safe," the great pitcher yelled. When the umpire walked away Dean hollered, "Well, at least answer me."

The umpire stopped and turned to face him. "I did," said the ump. "I shook my head."

"You couldn't have," argued Dizzy.

"Why not?" asked the umpire.

"Because if you did, I would have heard something rattle," answered Dizzy Dean.

GOOD-BYE

Babe Herman was a great hitter for the old Brooklyn Dodgers, but he wasn't the brightest guy in the world. Dodger owner Charlie Ebbets was so pleased with Herman's contribution to the club he offered him a free trip around the world. Babe wasn't impressed and replied, "Frankly, I'd prefer someplace else."

DOCTOR'S ORDERS

Dr. Franz Frisch was a noted medical specialist who loved the sport of baseball. He wasn't afraid to prescribe some fast remedies for umpires who in his opinion made bad calls. After complaining about a home-plate ump's decisions on balls and strikes inning after inning, the good doctor was finally confronted by the angry umpire. The ump tore off his mask, turned towards where Dr. Frisch was sitting, and yelled, "What did you say?"

Dr. Frisch was shocked only for a second. After a brief pause he yelled back, "Don't tell me you're deaf, too!"

NEVER SAY DIE

Archie Butt was a military aide to President William Howard Taft. In April of 1909, Butt persuaded President Taft to attend a Washington Senators baseball game. It was the first time any chief executive had ever made an appearance at America's national pastime. Late in the game, President Taft became concerned when the crowd grew angry and unruly due to some bad calls by the home-plate umpire. Mr. Butt quickly calmed him. "Don't worry, Mr. President," said Butt, "they never kill the umpire before the seventh inning."

NEW YORK SLAM

Some people think New York is a high-crime area. A visiting pro baseball player once said Shea Stadium is the only place you can get mugged on your way to second base.

TEAM EFFORT

The Chicago White Sox really stuck together in 1940. Everyone on the team had exactly the same batting average before and after opening day in 1940. That was because Bob Feller of the Cleveland Indians pitched a no-hitter and every Chicago player ended up with a .000 average until the next game.

SAY, WHAT?

Willie Mays of the San Francisco Giants was one of the greatest outfielders ever to play baseball. For a time, the right fielder who played beside Mays was Don Mueller. Don was a decent player who thought he was a great player and wasn't afraid to say so. "Willie, you've got it pretty soft in center," Don said to Mays one day. "You ought to try playing my position, right field."

Mays looked at Mueller. "I'm doing it now, every day," he answered with a chuckle.

TRUTH HURTS

Bill Mazeroski was one of the greatest second basemen to ever play major league baseball. However, when he first came into the major leagues he was a raw youngster who wasn't much of a hitter. He was very well liked despite his poor performance at the plate. "Mazeroski is a clean-cut, church-going youngster who is a model for all teenagers," a Pirate official told a sportswriter.

"That may be true," answered the writer, "but the Pirates might be better off with a juvenile delinquent who can hit."

PAIN KILLERS

The expansion New York Mets were so bad in 1962 that Manager Casey Stengel celebrated the rain-out of a doubleheader against the Milwaukee Braves by taking his team out for dinner. The Mets were so awful in their first major-league season that they won only 40 games while losing 120 games. When the season ended, Casey tried to cheer up his squad despite its dismal record. "Fellas," said Casey, "I don't want you to feel bad about this. This has been a team effort. No one or two players could have done all this." For some reason, his pep talk didn't really ease his players' pain.

FAMILY FEUD

In 1957, the New York Giants had a unique pitching combination on their staff. Pitcher Jim Davis was the nephew of pitcher Marv Grissom. When the Chicago Cubs played the Giants that year, Davis started on the mound, but the game had to be saved by Grissom. After the contest was over a Cub player had a great line. "At least," he said, referring to the loss, "we made them holler uncle."

DON'T MAKE WAVES

Pitcher Henry Heitman started on the mound for the Brooklyn Dodgers against the St. Louis Cardinals in 1918. After the first four batters he faced all got hits, Heitman was yanked out of the game. He was so mad he showered quickly and left the stadium in a huff. Then he joined the Navy and never played major league baseball again.

MUSCLE BOUND

Slugger Jimmie Foxx was one of baseball's greatest home-run hitters. Foxx weighed 195 pounds, and players who knew him said every pound was pure muscle. Pitcher Lefty Gomez once said, "Jimmie Foxx is so strong, he even has muscles in his hair!"

FRIENDLY COMPETITION

Bill Terry of the New York Giants had a lifetime batting average of .341, and was not popular with opposing pitchers. Dizzy Dean of the St. Louis Cardinals once said, "Could be that Bill Terry's a nice guy when you get to know him, but why bother?"

HOLY SMOKE

Pitcher Vernon Law was a very religious man, who always carried a Bible with him. Law was in a game pitching for the Pittsburgh Pirates when the opposing hurler knocked down a few Pirate batters with some very close pitches. "When that pitcher comes up," Pirate manager Danny Murtaugh said angrily to Law, "you knock him down with a pitch."

Vernon was shocked. He looked at his manager and reminded him, "The Bible says we should turn the other cheek, Skipper."

Law's comment did not extinguish Murtaugh's hot temper. "I know what the Bible says," Danny shouted, "and I say if you don't knock him down it's going to cost you a five-hundred-dollar fine."

Vernon Law didn't answer. When the opposing pitcher came to the plate, he knocked him down as directed. However, when he returned to the dugout at the end of the inning he said to Murtaugh, "The Bible also says he who lives by the sword shall perish by the sword."

YOGI BERRA GEMS

Half Witty

Yogi Berra was an All-Star catcher for the New York Yankees. He was also one of baseball's most colorful characters, who fired off a barrage of bizarre quotes during his sports career. While talking about baseball Yogi once said, "Ninety percent of this game is half mental."

Bat Mad

On one occasion, Yogi struck out on three pitches with the bases loaded. He tossed his bat into the dugout and remarked in disgust, "That bat ain't got no wood in it."

Holy Spoke

One day, Yogi was behind the plate when a batter stepped up and drew a cross in the dirt next to it for luck. Yogi stood up and rubbed out the cross with his shoe. "Why don't you just let God watch the game," said Yogi to the batter.

Money Mad

Everyone knew Yogi to be frugal with his money. Once a sportswriter asked him what he'd do if he found a million dollars. Said Yogi, "Well, if the guy who lost it was real poor, I'd give it back to him."

Headache

When Yogi reported to spring training early one season, the equipment manager asked him what his cap size was. "How should I know?" Yogi replied. "I'm not in shape yet."

Hand Signal

There was a pop-up down the third-base line between Yankee catcher Yogi Berra and third baseman Clete Boyer. The two players collided and the ball hit the ground. "Why didn't you yell for that ball?" Boyer grumbled to Berra. "I thought you could hear me waving at you," Yogi replied.

Irish Stew

Many years ago, Robert Briscoe, the mayor of the city of Dublin in Ireland, visited America. When Yogi was informed that Mr. Briscoe was the first Jewish mayor in Dublin history, he exclaimed, "Isn't that wonderful! It could only happen in America."

WORLD-CLASS CHUCKLES

PRIZE FIGHT

World heavyweight boxing champion John L. Sullivan was a hot-tempered man who didn't always confine his fights to the ring. He once got into an argument with a streetcar conductor who wouldn't allow him to take his pet dog on the trolley. In the heat of the moment, Sullivan socked the conductor and ended up getting arrested. The heavyweight champ was brought before a judge who wasn't impressed with John's title. "Mr. Sullivan, I fine you one hundred dollars for hitting that man," said the judge. "Do you have anything to say to that?"

The great John L. reached for his wallet and replied. "Yes, your honor. I'll give you another two hundred if you'll let me hit him again."

PACHYDERM PACERS

In 1980, a quarter-mile race called the "Elephantonian" was held at Monticello Raceway (for horses) in the United States. The race matched a six-year-old, 3,000-pound elephant against an eight-year-old, 3,500-pound elephant named Nellie. Who won? Tusk! Tusk! The results were never reported.

PLANE MIX-UP

When West German soccer star Karl-Heinz Granitza played for the Chicago Sting, he had a language problem. Granitza was unable to read or speak English and that had some hilarious results. Once when the Chicago team was flying out of Chicago for an away game, he made a mistake and got on the wrong airplane. As the plane started to taxi away from the terminal, he noticed that none of his fellow players or coaches were aboard. Quickly he realized he'd made a big error. Jumping out of his seat, he shouted at the top of his lungs in German for the plane to stop moving immediately. The plane did stop, but not because it had a celebrity soccer player aboard. Everyone thought Granitza was a would-be hijacker. Luckily for him, the case of mistaken intentions was sorted out shortly afterwards.

TO COIN A PHRASE

A soccer official got the captains of two second-grade soccer teams on the field for a coin toss before the contest. "When I flip this coin, you call it," the official said to one of the youngsters, a boy with red hair. The boy nodded. The official flipped the coin.

"Quarter!" the red-headed boy shouted.

SUPER WHO?

Many people believed that super-boxer Muhammad Ali had an ego that matched his vast talent in the ring. Although few opposing boxers could ever cut Ali down to size, an airline stewardess on a flight from Washington to New York once did that quite easily. She went up to Muhammad Ali as the plane prepared for takeoff. "Mr. Ali, please fasten your seat belt."

Ali stared at her and answered, "Superman don't need no seat belt."

The stewardess took his response in stride. Calmly she replied, "Superman don't need no plane, either!"

HERE'S TO YOU

A wise guy reporter once asked NHL goalie Gump Worsley, then of the Minnesota North Stars, if it was true that he did all of his training in St. Paul bars. Gump grinned and replied, "Not so! I've switched to Minneapolis." He was of course referring to St. Paul's sister city.

HUNGRY FOR A WIN

The Toronto Maple Leafs suffered through some tough defeats during the 1991–92 season. After one particularly hard loss to swallow, Coach Tom Watt had this to say to reporters, "If it had been raining soup, we would have had forks!"

HORSE SENSE

Whoa! Would you believe that Olympic track immortal Jessie Owens once raced a horse? It's true. When Owens decided to become a professional runner, he raced a horse named Julio McCaw at a racetrack in Havana, Cuba, as a publicity stunt. The race turned out to be funny to everyone but the horse. Owens was awarded a 40-yard handicap in the 100-yard race and won! The last laugh was on Julio McCaw.

MISSING LINKS

Pro golfer Gary Player is very attached to his special putter. The putter and player have been together for some 30 years, which is longer than most modern marriages last. When asked about his attachment to the putter, Gary joked, "If I had to choose between my wife and my putter . . . well, I'd miss her."

DRESSING DOWN

One sunny afternoon at the Hillcrest Golf Club, famous old-time comedians Harpo Marx and George Burns were playing a round of golf. The sun was so hot that day that Harpo and George decided to take off their shirts. When a club official saw the two men playing shirtless, he ran after them and began to holler. "You can't do that! It's against the club rules," he yelled. "Put your shirts back on!"

"Do we have to?" asked George Burns.

"Absolutely," the official insisted. "I told you. The rules state all golfers on this course have to wear shirts."

Burns shrugged. "Okay," he said, and they put their shirts back on. As soon as the official was gone, however, the two comedians took off their pants and started to finish their round wearing only their undershorts. When the official turned and spotted them walking off in their undershorts, he lost his temper. "What are you doing?" he yelled as he ran after them again.

"The rules state we have to play with shirts on, right?" asked George Burns.

"R-r-right," sputtered the official.

"Is there any written rule that states we have to play with pants on?"

The club official thought for a moment. "Well," he muttered. "No."

"Then leave us alone and go away," Burns ordered as he walked off with Harpo Marx.

MAROONED

NHL hockey star Pat Price was asked whom he'd like to be marooned on a desert island with. Price replied, "One of my old coaches . . . I'd kill him." However, Pat never did name the coach he had in mind.

HIT OR MISS

An old golf story claims that United States President Ulysses S. Grant once took a trip to Scotland with a friend. While there, Grant's friend took him to a golf course to show him how the game was played. Grant stood by quietly and watched a golfer at work. The golfer took a mighty swing, missed the ball, and tore up a chunk of turf. The golfer tried again. He missed and another divet was sent sailing through the air. After several more hard swings and near misses, Grant turned to his host. "The game seems to result in a considerable amount of exercise," he said. "But would you mind telling me what the ball is for?"

MONEY TALKS

In 1960, the Toronto Maple Leafs met the Detroit Red Wings in the first round of the Stanley Cup playoffs. After the Wings won the first game of the best of five series, Punch Imlach, the general manager of the Leafs, decided his club needed a pep talk before Game Two.

Instead of talking to his players, Imlach wrote the squad a message on the dressing-room blackboard. The players came into the locker room after their pregame warm-up and saw these words: "Take at look at the center of the floor. This represents the difference between winning and losing." When they looked at the center of the locker-room floor they saw a pile of money amounting to over one thousand dollars. Inspired by the loot before them, the Toronto Maple Leafs went out and won the game and eventually the semi-final playoffs.

HOT DOG! A WIENER!

There are so many sports today that it had to happen. In 1994, a sporting event really went to the dogs, and the dogs were racing dachshunds. At Multnomah Greyhound Park in Portland, Oregon, 32 dachshunds competed in a 100-yard dash for the gold. The winner of the race, a hot dog named Rudy, earned a year's supply of free dog food for his effort. By the way, the name of the competition was the Wiener Dog Summer Nationals.

FISHY STORY

They say that American humorist Mark Twain was a great sportsman and outdoorsman. Twain especially loved hunting and fishing. One day he was on a train bound for New York after spending three weeks in the wilds of New England. As the train pulled out of a depot in Maine, an elderly gentleman sat down next to Twain.

"Have you been out in the woods?" the gentleman asked in an attempt to strike up some polite conversation.

"I sure have," stated Twain proudly. "And let me tell you something. It may be closed season up here in Maine for fishing, but I have a hundred pounds of the finest bass you ever saw iced down in the baggage car and headed for home with me." Mark Twain glanced at the old New Englander. "And just who are you, sir?" he asked.

"Me?" answered the gentleman as he eyed Twain suspiciously. "I'm a Maine game warden, sir. And who are you?"

Twain gulped. "Warden," he replied, "I'm the biggest liar in the entire United States."

HARD KNOCK!

During a really physical NHL game between the Boston Bruins and the New York Islanders, the Islanders' captain was knocked to the ice and just lay there. "Look at that!" an Islander player said to the referee. "A Bruin player hit our captain with a stick and knocked him unconscious. One of their players deserves a misconduct penalty!"

"Baloney!" yelled the Bruins' captain. "This is a trick." He pointed at the unconscious Islander. "He didn't get hit with a stick, he was knocked out by the puck."

Hearing that, the Islander captain raised himself up on the ice and shouted, "It was a stick that knocked me unconscious!" And then he lay back down.

CHURCH STEEPLECHASE

Many years ago there was a great American track runner named Gil Dodds. Gil was an ordained minister and because of that he was nicknamed "the Flying Parson." One day after he had defeated a highly regarded competitor, the two runners were interviewed by a reporter. "To what do you owe your success in today's race?" the reporter asked Dodds.

Not wanting to take personal credit for his feat, Dodds replied, "The Lord ran with me today."

The reporter then turned to Dodds's competitor. "What happened to you?" the reporter asked. "Can you explain your loss?"

"I sure can," answered the competitor. "I had to run all alone out there."

STRIKE OUT

Bowling is a popular sport in America, but don't bet on it. Betting on the game of bowling almost finished it as a sport. In the 1840's, Connecticut lawmakers banned it because too much gambling went on when people bowled. To stop the gambling, nine-pin bowling was made illegal. To get around the law, bowlers added a tenth pin so they could bowl without breaking the law. Bowling has been using ten pins ever since.

WORD TO THE WISE

High-school cross-country runner Morgan Pellowski wasn't his team's greatest runner, but he was always fast with a quick-witted response. When Morgan switched from soccer to cross country, his young coach gave him and other new runners a big pep talk at the start of the season. "In cross country," said the coach, "winning the race is not the most important thing. To be a good long distance runner, you have to be determined and dedicated. A cross-country runner never gives up. Always finish the race. Don't be a quitter."

The season began and Morgan didn't win a lot of races, but he finished every one. Around mid-season, he took an after-school job to make extra money. From time to time he had to get permission from his cross-country coach to leave practice early so he could arrive at his new job on time. Finally, the coach tired of excusing Morgan from practice and told him he'd have to give up his after-school job if he wanted to stay on the team.

"But, coach," he protested, "I can't. After all, a cross-country runner never quits," he reminded his mentor. All the members of the team laughed, and so did the coach. Morgan was granted permission to keep his after-school job.

ROYAL DISRESPECT

The 1980, Winter Olympics were held at Lake Placid in the United States. Celebrities from all over the world attended the games. Among the notables on hand were King Gustav and Queen Silvia of Sweden. One evening the royal couple went to an Olympic skating event and found out they'd brought the wrong tickets with them. A guard at the gate to the ice arena refused to admit them to the event.

"But you don't understand," Gustav said. "I am the king of Sweden."

The guard just sneered and shook his head. "Oh, right," he replied and then pointed to Gustav's wife. "And next you'll be telling me she's the queen!"

NOT LETTER PERFECT

Boxer Mike Tyson knew his way around a ring, but couldn't always handle the punchline in an interview. There's a Tyson story about a sportswriter who sat down to ask the heavyweight champ a few questions. "I'm from the U.P.I. [United Press Information] wire service," the reporter said.

Tyson nodded. "One of your trucks ran over my dog," he said.

"No, no, Mike," whispered one of Tyson's associates, "that was U.P.S. [United Parcel Service, a delivery company]."

SEEING DOUBLE

Karl Meiler of West Germany lost a World Cup tennis match to an American player named Gullikson in 1977. Gullikson beat Meiler playing right-handed. Two weeks later Meiler found himself across the net from Gullikson again. But this time, Gullikson played left-handed and beat him. "What's happening to me?" Meiler exclaimed after the disappointing loss. "This American Gullikson can beat me playing with either hand."

Meiler was slightly relieved to learn that he'd lost the first match to Tim Gullikson, a right-handed player, and the second match to Tim's twin brother, Tom Gullikson, a left-handed player.

NIGHTMARE

Prior to the 1957 Kentucky Derby, racehorse owner Ralph Lowe had a bad dream. He dreamed that his colt Gallant Man, one of the Derby favorites, was racing down the homestretch when the rider misjudged the finish line and pulled up, costing Gallant Man the race. Lowe told Gallent Man's jockey, Bill Shoemaker, about his nightmare. Shoemaker just laughed and told Ralph Lowe to forget about silly stuff like dreams. Then on Derby day Bill Shoemaker went out, misjudged the finish line, and stood up in the stirrups at the 16th pole, causing Gallant Man to finish second to Iron Liege by a nose.

NOTE THIS

On occasion, celebrities who are asked to sing the national anthem before a sporting event in the United States simply goof up the words. When a singer flubs the words of *The Star Spangled Banner,* no one in America makes a big deal out of it. However, in Mexico a celebrity who botches the singing of *Himno Nacional de Mexico* does not always get off as easy. In 1989, Mexican pop singer Jorge Muniz goofed up the words of the Mexican anthem before a boxing match in Mexico City and paid a heavy price for his mistakes. Mexican officials were so angered by Muniz's performance that the singer was fined one million pesos for "disrespect for national symbols."

NUTTY NAMES, FUNNY FACTS, AND WACKY RULES

GUN SHY

In the late 1940's, the old Brooklyn Dodgers baseball team had three outfielders who were really sons of a gun—thanks to their nicknames. The players were Tommy "Buckshot" Brown, George "Shotgun" Shuba, and Carl "the Reading Rifle" Furillo.

ODDBALL HANDLE

First baseman Dick Stuart of the Pittsburgh Pirates was such a terrible fielder that teammates nicknamed him "Dr. Strangeglove."

GROW UP

NHL hockey player Butch Goring was nicknamed "Seed" by his teammates due to his questionable hygiene habits. On occasion, Goring's attire wasn't very fresh, and when he traveled with the squad he sometimes took only a toothbrush on lengthy road trips.

OPPOSITE ENDS

In 1973, a high-school basketball team in Bellefontaine, Ohio, had a 5-foot, 10-inch guard named Long and a 6-foot, 5-inch center named Short.

SAW ENOUGH

NFL linebacker Jack Reynolds acquired his nickname "Hacksaw" in an unusual way. When he was a senior college player at the University of Tennessee, his team was upset by the University of Mississippi. Reynolds was so mad that after the game he took a hacksaw and sawed an old '53 Chevy (that had no motor) right in half.

CATCH SOME Z's

Pitcher William "Sleepy Bill" Burns was a notorious major league goldbrick. He got his nickname because on the days he didn't pitch he sat on the bench and slept through the game, and on the days he did pitch he only dozed between innings.

ALLEY CATS

The following are all professional bowlers who don't need snazzy nicknames because of their real names. They are: Curv Rohler, Billy Lane, Dale Strike, Paul Boehler, and Dave Frame.

YAWN!

In 1981, Dick Dull was the University of Maryland's athletic director, while Les Boring played tackle on the Maryland football team.

PLAYER PROBLEM

In the early days of football, the game did not have a lot of standard rules. Originally, there was no rule governing how many players could actively participate on each side. Before a game, the two teams involved decided how many players would be on the field at one time. On occasion, as many as 25 players on each side played in early football contests. It wasn't until 1876 that a rule was established limiting each team to just 15 players on the field. Finally, in 1880 the rule was changed to allow teams the use of only 11 players at a time.

FOUL RULE

A foul ball in baseball was not always counted as a strike. It wasn't until 1895 that a rule was passed in major league baseball that made a foul ball a strike.

FLAGGED

Up until 1965, official National Football League penalty flags were white, not yellow. On April 5, 1965, a rule changed the color of penalty flags used in NFL games from white to yellow.

GET THE POINT?

A notice was posted in the lobby of the Chicago Athletic Club that read: "Join our fencing team—we need some new blood."

CLEVELAND CHAOS

The Cleveland Indians baseball team was once known as the Cleveland Spiders because most of the team's players were tall and skinny. The team was later called the Blues or Bluebirds. In 1902, it was known as the Cleveland Broncos. In 1903, it was called the Naps in honor of its star player, Napoleon "Naps" Lajoie. In 1914, the Cleveland team finally became known as the Indians in honor of star Spiders player Louis "Chief" Socklexis, who was a member of the Penobscot tribe.

ON TRACK

The following names are of lady athletes who once competed in legitimate track meets around the United States: Terry Christmas, Betta Little, Beverly Hill, Ingrid Sprint, and Merri Furlong.

NYUK! NYUK!

In 1990, the three referees at a recreation basketball game in Stevens Point, Wisconsin, were named Jim Moe, Larry Kokkeler, and Curly Marguard.

GOD'S HONEST TRUTH

A Methodist Church in Houston, Texas, sponsored a bowling league in 1965. One of the teams in the league was called "The Holy Rollers."

POPULAR NAME

Basketball coach Larry Murphy of Allagash High School in Maine had a name problem when it came to the players on his squad in 1978. Of the 13 players on the Allagash High squad that season, six had the last name Kelly and three had the last name McBreairty.

PASSING GRADE

When you want to move the ball down the court in basketball, you can either dribble or pass. Many years ago, basketball players did not have that choice. Why not? Dribbling in basketball was once an illegal maneuver. When the game was invented in 1891, only passing was allowed. It wasn't until around 1900 that a rule change made dribbling a ball legal.

SLIPUP

Many years ago, there was a minor-league hockey team called the Macon Whoopees.

DOT'S NICE

A high-school football team in Poca, West Virginia, decided on an interesting name for its squad—the Poca Dots!

WHO?

Connie Mack is a famous name in baseball history. He won fame as a big league player and manager. However, his real name was Cornelius McGillicuddy. It was shortened to Connie Mack when he was a youngster growing up in Massachusetts.

HANDS OFF

Ouch! Prior to 1914, hockey officials were required to *place* the puck down on the ice between players' sticks for face-offs. More often than not, officials ended up with broken hands, cut fingers, and bruised bones. To save them some pain, a rule was finally passed in 1914 that allowed them to simply drop the puck between the sticks of players for face-offs.

HAIL TO THE CHIEF

On February 17, 1992, college basketball teams from George Washington and James Madison Universities met on the court to play a game. The match appropriately occurred on the American holiday known as Presidents' Day.

UNIFORM PAY

The pre-Columbian Aztecs in Mexico played a game similar to basketball which they called *ollamalitzil*. Players in the game tried to put a solid-rubber ball through a hole in a fixed stone ring placed high on the side of a stadium wall. Losing a game of *ollamalitzil* was costly. The captain of the losing squad was often beheaded and the winning team was entitled to the clothing of all of the spectators as a prize for being victorious.

CHEER FEAR

Who invented cheerleaders? Many sports historians believe the first cheerleaders were used by Princeton University in 1869 and 1870. In 1869, Princeton and Rutgers Universities met in New Jersey to play the first college football game in history. Part of Princeton's team strategy was to have its players yell loudly during the game to distract and frighten the opposition. The strategy didn't quite work, as Princeton lost that first game in 1869. All that yelling also wore out the Princeton players. However, the next year, the team brought a special group of spectators to the contest to do the yelling and cheering for them. In 1870, with the help of its special "cheerleaders," Princeton defeated Rutgers on the gridiron.

A STROKE OF BAD LUCK

The game of golf was so popular in Scotland during the 15th century that King James II was afraid it would replace archery in popularity among his people. Since archery was necessary for national defense, the king outlawed the sport, and it wasn't until 1502 that it was legal to play golf in Scotland once again.

BEST REST

The final resting place of William Ambrose Hulbert, who helped found baseball's National League, is in Chicago near Wrigley Field. The tombstone is in the shape of a large baseball.

DARN SOX

The Red Sox, of baseball's American League, had some interesting name changes over the years. The team was originally called the Plymouth Rocks. The word Rocks was dropped, and over the years the squad was known as the Pilgrims, the Puritans, and then the Somersets. In 1907, it was renamed the Boston Red Stockings, and in 1908 finally dubbed the Boston Red Sox.

WHO ARE YOU?

Early in his boxing career, middleweight Mustafa Hamsho had a tough time finding opponents. Mustafa had a reputation and a name that struck fear in the hearts of would-be adversaries. In order to get fights, Mustafa had to schedule fights under the monikers Rocky Estafire and Mike Astifire. He later went back to fighting under his real name.

MEAN GREEN

Donnybrook is a suburb of Dublin where an annual fair was held for more than 600 years. The fair was discontinued in 1855 due to the violent brawls that always broke out while it was going on. The word Donnybrook is now used as a slang term in sports as a synonym for brawl.

ALLEY WHO?

Historians believe the ancient Egyptians enjoyed the sport of bowling. Pieces of stone used as pins and a stone ball used to knock the pins down were found in the tomb of an Egyptian child.

JUST FOR KICKS

When the game of basketball was invented in 1891, there were no "basketballs," so soccer balls were used to play the game. It wasn't until 1894 that a special "basketball" was first introduced. A "laceless" basketball came into use in 1937, and the modern basketball appeared in 1950.

CARDINAL SIN

The St. Louis Cardinals, of baseball's National League, were known as the St. Louis Perfectos from 1899 to 1900.

I SEE YOU

It's not always easy to name children. Ronald Wayne Street and his wife, Dee, didn't decide on a name for their daughter until she was three years old. Finally, the free-spirited couple decided to call their little girl "Picabo." Picabo is pronounced just like the game "peek-a-boo" which parents play with their infants. Picabo Street grew up to be a skier who won a silver medal in the Women's Downhill at the 1994 Olympics.

Picabo claims her brother Ron almost ended up with a name equally as interesting as her own. Her dad was going to name him Juan Way Street, but in the end he settled for plain old Ron.

FRANKLY, WHO CARES?

Johnny Franks was the sports information director at Tennessee State University in the early 1990's. His nickname was Johnny "Ball Park" Franks. He picked it up during his days working for a minor league baseball team.

INDEX

ABOUT THE AUTHOR

Michael Morgan Pellowski lives with a family of athletes. Michael went to Rutgers College on a football scholarship and won seven letters in football and baseball. In baseball, he posted a .314 career average. He was defensive captain of the football team and won A.P. and E.C.A.C. All-East honors. He also had pro football tryouts in the NFL and CFL.

Michael's wife, Judy, ran cross country and track in college. Their son Morgan won five letters in soccer, cross country and track, and was a cross country co-captain. He also played baseball and basketball. Son Matthew plays football, baseball, and basketball, and also ran cross country. Daughter Melanie plays softball and basketball, runs cross country, and is a cheerleader. Son Martin plays soccer, basketball, and baseball.